Meeting Needs

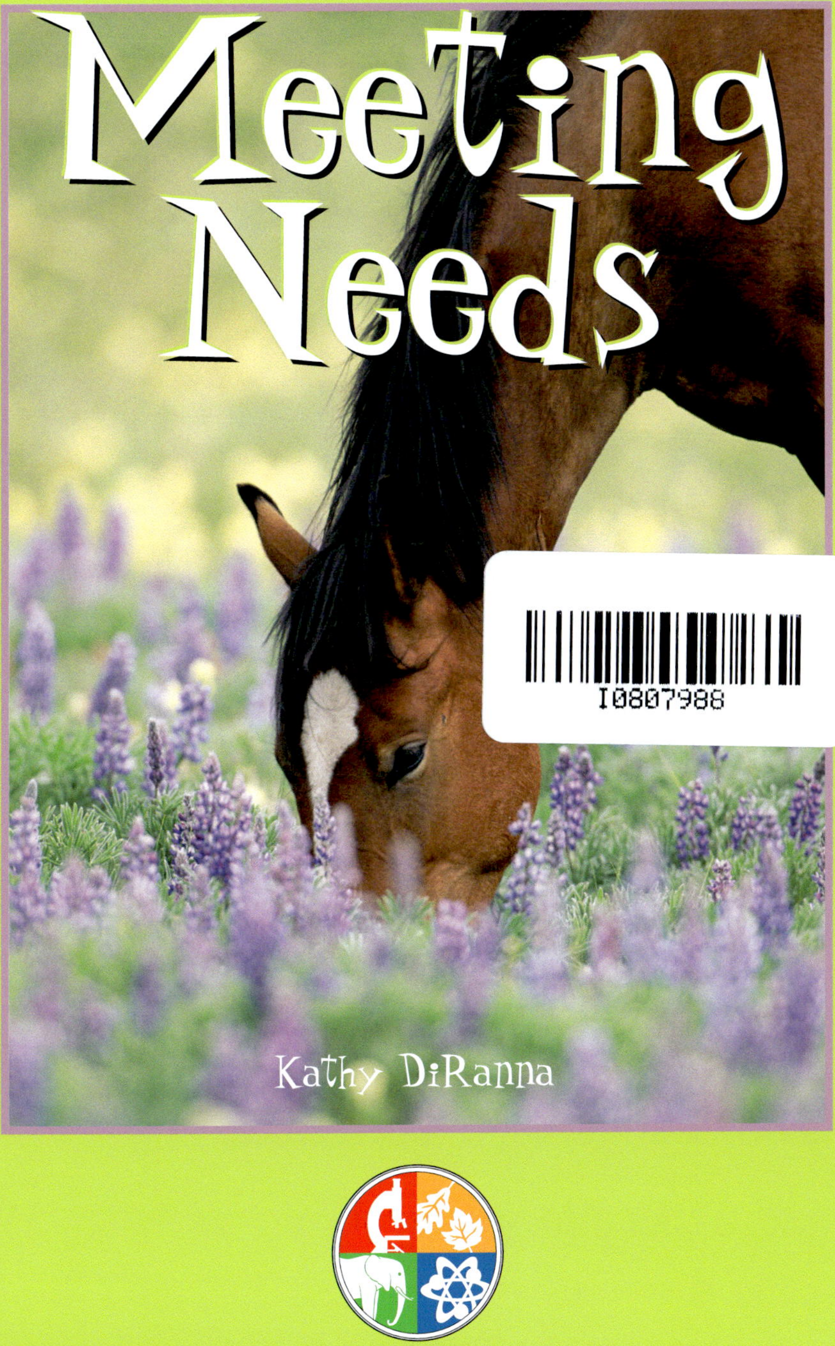

Kathy DiRanna

Rosen Classroom Books & Materials™
New York

Living things need food, water, air, and a place to stay safe.

Living things use their environment to meet their needs.

Animals get food from many places.

A hawk has a sharp **beak** to hunt small animals.

Some whales use their mouths to strain food from the water.

Plants make their own food from sunlight, water, and gases in the air.

Many people get food from the **grocery store**.

Some people grow their own vegetables and fruits and raise their own animals.

Many animals have lungs to breathe air. Some animals have **gills** to breathe in the water.

Animals use their environment to make their homes. Birds build **nests**, **gophers** make **burrows**, bears use caves, and humans build houses.

Words to Know

beak

burrow

gills

gopher

grocery store

nest